ABOUT THE AUTHOR

Dr. Karthik Raj R is a MBBS graduate hailing from Kerala. He has been well known in the field of medical academics by being Record Holder in "India Book of Records" for being the youngest medical blogger in India. He moved into the literature world with his first book named 'Triangle of life', which was published under his pen name Ankith Krishnan. He had already published a 2nd part of 'Triangle of Life'- which was a popular short stories amoung the domestic competitions. His vision is to make the reader obtain a cinematic view for the story and get the readers get going through emotions. His stories are focused on family emotions, friendship and romance. He has a strong admiration for the sports and among them, he is a great enthusiast of football. He aims to bridge the gap of literature and visual media by his work and in future he believes that he can make his work full fledged in the form of visual media like webseries or movies. He is also a strong advocate of mental health and he has worked in various social campaigns supporting mental health. You can find him at Instagram in the name- 'Confused_doc_official'.

English Language
Capitano
Story of a CR7 Fan Boy
(Novel)
by
Dr. Karthik

Published in October 2024
by Decan Imprint Publishing Co.
Reg. Off: Sharjah Publishing City
Free Zone Sharjah, UAE.
Phone: 00971-551830334
Email : decanimprint@gmail.com

Cover Design : Watermelon

19/24-25/Sl.No.19/50/NS 15.4
ISBN 978-93-5973-517-7

Capitano

Story of a CR7 Fan Boy

Dr. Karthik

DECANIMPRINT

Goals

I
Prologue

I could not believe the noise around me. I didn't know whether it was a dream for me to be here. But the only thing I knew was to reach India from Spain as fast as possible. Because the person that keeps me motivating was wanting me there. It had been 2 months since I left India to the great Madrid. It was a warm morning in Madrid and I was tired after a long heavy load of work. I woke up listening to my alarm, after 8.00 AM in the morning. The view was really beautiful in the balcony. I went with my coffee to the balcony to enjoy the view. It was the moment I received the message from my Arundathi. I couldn't believe my eye. The message was that she was getting married and she could not accept anyone other than me. The message was delivered a month ago. I found it after 3 and half weeks. The date of marriage was 3 days from now on. I don't know what I could do. I couldn't really give her to someone she doesn't love. This was the moment I felt that with her, everything was perfect in my life. I packed my bag very fast as I had only 3 days to reach there. I called my superior and told that I wanted to leave for my country I will be back soon. But he told me, "remember Arun, its one of the important announcement we had to make. We can't delay any more than 2 days."

" Sir, its important", I told what was the matter. When he heard it, he told me that this is one of the thing that should be delivered at the day of my meeting with my girl.

"Go on my boy bring her back and make her yours officially, we will be waiting for you."

I suddenly searched for flight tickets and ordered my ticket for tomorrow. That left me two day before marriage. I could not sleep the whole day thinking of her and the most memorable moments that happened between me and her. I miss her most during these times. I felt both happy and sad at the same time. I somehow managed to sleep for about 2 hours. My superior told me before dropping me at the airport, "Arun we will be waiting…for it."

"I know sir. I won't delay more than 2 days."

I walked, thinking about her to airport check in. The next thing I knew, I was in the plane. One of the co passenger sitting next to me was shouting like hell. He was shouting to the mobile while playing top eleven. "Come on pass you idiot! Where the hell do you think you pass your ball." I was just looking at the screen and he was an English person. I told him, "Sir, you are playing a side of most high defensive formation and you are hoping that putting an attacking formation while using flanks will work in this case. Sir just let me tell your opposing team is having a high defensive line. So I suggest you should try to push the opposition defense forward from the high defensive line to move up the field by using a skill full secondary striker and cutting inward wing forwards. The skilful player will hold the ball from defensive line and will make the wing forwards, mask from the defense and you will get the right pass to your forward and bang Goal……Just set this instruction and you will be fine."

"Ok let me try this, if I fail you had to give me 10 bucks."

"Ok sir, I accept the bet", I said. After a short time, he told me that they won 4-2 and they we were lagging 2-1 in first half. "You really know your stuff kid. Actually who are you?", he asked me.

"Sir, I am a.."

"Yes, let me guess you are a football gamer. Yes I knew that you are good at this."

"Sir I'm.."

"Actually, don't tell me I know u don't have to give me 10 bucks. I will give you something special, new Sporting Club jersey. Actually, you know Ronaldo is taking his share at the club and taking over. Wonder what changes will he be doing."

"Yes sir, I am a huge fan of him. I went to Spain to see the ceremony of his announcement."

"Wow that's cool", he said. "So why the hurrying back from the ceremony. As I hope tomorrow is the function."

"Yes sir but I have to reach my homeland for my girl."

"Why hurry mister?"

"Sir she is getting married to someone else whom she doesn't like. I have to reach there and stop it."

"Oh that's great! So, I guess there is a beautiful love story to be heard in this light journey. There is about 3 hours remaining for your destination. So, just tell your lovely love story to me."

"Sorry Sir, this is not about a girl and how she got into my life. It is all because of a much more important reason that even the two of us became close. The one reason that even made us talk this much longer. Football, the one reason that changed my life and the one person in football I owed it to the most", I said.

"Who is that?", he asked.

"Sir, you gave me the jersey of a football club. The person that made the club legendary. None other than the greatest machine footballer of all time, Cristiano Ronaldo. The one I always admired and the one I always felt so close to my life. And the words which make every fan goes wild , Siiiiii………..! Sir, this is the basis of my story."

He told me that before he actually wanted to hear the story he thought it was a boring usual romantic story. But now it is a big deal. "Just tell me the whole story I am listening all of it whatever happens. Please tell, man."

"Yes sir, I will."

"I can't wait to see what unfolds between football and romance. What happened and what made up to the current situation."

He was staring at me like a curious guy and I was just smiling and looking at him and just in my mind refreshing through my world. The world of a CR7 fan boy.

II
Beginning of a true fan

This story starts in a small Mumbai street where my dad, Mr.Raghavan, worked as a personal secretary for a great mobile manufacturing company and my mother worked as a cashier in government run state bank. They were both a happily married couple with me and my sister Nandini. We were a middle class family but my parents never made me suffer for each second they let me follow anything I want. My Nandini was more than a great sister to me, she is my motivation syrup. She supported me in everything and take blame for everything I did. I was really happy to have her as my sister.

During my initial childhood we were having black and white television and we used to watch movies and Indian cricket matches in our local channel. But I remember it was a festival when our first colour television came to my house. Me and my sister were waiting after the school even without changing uniform to watch our first colour television. And about 6:00 PM evening my father arrived with TV and mechanic along side with him. We were watching it very carefully like children watching candy shop keepers placing candy in their shops. We were so restless to see our colour television. It was getting late and my mother forced me and my sister to have a bath and without our full mind we went to take a quick bath and return. But we were unfortunate that we couldn't see the TV on that day as the electricity in our village has gone after 8.00PM and will come by tomorrow morning only. We were devastated that night as we couldn't watch the TV on that day and all the next day in the school both me and my sister were thinking of only watching our TV. At last, after our school got over, we rushed to our home to watch TV. And my mother knew that we were ready to watch the TV and she was in our doorsteps and she gave the remote to me and told me that watch all you like today and I will prepare your evening snack. My sister was furious that she didn't get the remote and finally we accept to press a channel number randomly and we will be forced to watch it. We pressed a no. 37 and both against my sister's cartoon wish and my superhero TV shows, there came a sports channel where a group of players were assembling in a big stadium and a person in a black t shirt was coming out of a tunnel and group of red shirts and a green and white mixed t shirt individuals come out of the tunnel. Due to the colour fantasy me and my sister were watching it without even knowing what that meant. My sister cheered when red boys get the ball and I cheered when green and white boys take the ball and suddenly out of nowhere I noticed a curly green hair individual with lean body was moving the ball like anything. I was simply watching him all the game without blinking. His movement with the ball mesmerised me as he was so lean but his skills were so mad that I was just so immersed and it was around 5 PM and our dad came and take the remote and told us he want to watch the news. We both resisted but our dad forcefully sent us to do our homework and take a bath. When I returned after doing homework and bath I checked the tv channel but there was no game and there was some people discussing about some news. I was so sad I couldn't see the green hair guy. But at that night there was lot of balloons in my house. I fill the balloon with air and me and my sister started to play. We both played with our foot. We played this till our bedtime, even when my mother forced me to go to sleep. But I couldn't sleep that night thinking of him and his skills. In that night I decided that I want to become like that guy.

In the next day, one of the sight which conquered my mind was there right in front of my eyes. As some of the students were playing the ball game which I watched last night. I was waiting for the class to get over with to get a touch for the ball. I was eagerly waiting at the touch line for chance to play. As I gathered the courage to ask them to play with me. But there was this guy who always there as an opposition to me, James who is the son of a famous rich entrepreneur, who consider this as the opportunity to get a ball boy instead of giving me a chance. I didn't know watching them play had made the time past 6 pm in the evening. Once the game was finishing, I looked at my watch and saw the time and now I realised that my dad will be really angry at me and I went running to my home. There was my sister and mom staring at me when I returned home. I saw dad with a huge stick waiting for me. The rest was painful thrashing for an hour even without getting a chance to explain what happened. Even while I was in 9th standard, Dad never allowed to me stay at school for long time. At last I got a chance to explain the reason which I thought will reduce my thrashing but it didn't stop there it continued but I don't know why I didn't feel that much pain even while I was getting thrashed but I was getting thrilled at my first football experience at the field as a ball boy which I really enjoyed. Even though I didn't felt pain at that time but later that night it was a difficult night to sleep. At night I saw my father came and ask me "did it pain son?"

I replied, "no dad it didn't pain when you hit at that time.

But now its hurting." Dad then put the painkiller ointments on my leg and arms and massaged me for quite some time. After that he told me that if I am interested in playing the game after school I stay there after school but don't come home alone. I don't know that after I heard those words I just hugged my dad for a long time. I don't know whether the pain killers relieved my pain or words from my father. I was really enjoying the night. All I could imagine was tomorrow evening time as I could get a chance to enter the field.

As days passed I became a regular ball boy at the field. After a few days I was restless to get on the field. I desperately ask my senior James who was the captain of my school team to ask me to play with them. He asked me to play as a defender at the right position. I told him that, "brother I want to play as a striker. He looked at me and said, "you didn't even get a chance to touch the ball. You don't have a field experience for a minute. Just remember I am the captain here and I decide the things here. You just obey it or you can just leave."

I just told sorry and I told him that I will play in any position all I wanted was to play in the field. As the game progressed, the ball finally went to my side. And the first touch of the ball I received at my feet. I felt like marching towards with the ball. With the first touch I started doing some skills with the ball and marched forward then James who was in the opposite team with just a push had the ball with him and he stopped the play. "Who the bloody f*** are you? Pele, Mara Dona, Messi or Ronaldo. Trying to show off you bloody bitch. You are not getting a second chance again. Get out of here", he told me.

I begged him but he pushed me to the side line. I was really devastated and there was my second trouble in the form of a friend named Karan who I meant trouble is because that his affection towards me always landed me in trouble. But our meeting in that pitch was rather very funny. I was sitting in the side-lines and he came to me and told that your footwork was amazing but you need to perfect it. I listened to him very carefully as he was some genius. But later one senior came to him said, "hey water boy give us some water." He rushed to give them water, after he returned I asked, "you know better than me in every aspect. Why did they make you water boy and not even ball boy?"

He told me that the person with talent will never be recognised. I replied, "true that bro."

"Hey Skillzzz!"

Some sweet voice was heard from behind me. It was a beautiful girl who was sitting behind me after tennis practice. And there was my second love Arundathi with whom I fell in love instantly after watching her but I didn't have the courage to tell her my love. And he told me that, "hey you fool do u believe that someone who is worth a talent should be sitting as a water boy?" She told me that he put a goal in his own net and was kicked out of the field. I just watched him and he was telling me that how can we know that which is the correct goal post. I just looked at him and I laughed and we both laughed at each other. Then we saw the batch from the side line and the match came to end at 6.00 PM. Me and Karan stood up from the ground and walked towards the gate where my father was standing there. I introduced Karan to my father and we were talking. As I realised that my father was rushing to a person and was talking to him with respect. Suddenly Arundathi came to me and called my name, "Arun, you had nice skills and touch I think you should watch more games and practice then you will be perfect." I asked her that how did she know about my name. She replied that she knows everything about me and I ask how then she told me that because of that man and she just suddenly walked off. And that man was the person who was talking to my father. I asked my father while returning home who was that person he was talking to. He replied that he was his boss and I was working as a personal assistant to him. He told me that he had only one daughter and she was studying in my class. And he told me that she was like a daughter to him and that he used to take care of her in childhood. I asked him, "Dad, did you tell anything about me?" And he replied, "she knows everything about you, son." I decided that day, may be this was a God's gift that I could get a chance to become friends with her.

Even while thinking of her my mind was always dissolved in football but I also felt that with her, I conquer more. I slept with lots of beautiful memories in my mind. I woke up early morning and decided to have a little physical exercise to shape my body and after that I went to school. I went straight to class and there was my friend Karan waiting with a vacant seat for me. I sat next to him and I was about to tell that I wanted to talk to her but at the same time he asked me, "did u like Arundathi?" I was shell shocked that how did he get it. I told him, "boss you are genius."

He nodded at me like that was nothing. He told me, "you should become close friends with her and later confess your feelings."

I tell him "no way bro! I can't tell her that I love her. She is my father's boss's daughter. I know but before I tell her I want something to prove to her. She will not accept me because I am a nobody to her. I want to become something in front of her before confessing my feelings."

Karan also nodded at me. Then Arundathi suddenly came to the class room and I was like suddenly I don't know what to do and I started doing stupid things and Karan asked me, "what happened to you, bro? Any fits or something? Hey just behave normal in front of her do not make her realise that you are just a delicate person in front of her. Be brave."

And I stored all my courage in front of her and nodded her a hi. She just nodded a hi to me. By that time I was in a lot of sweat and he just had a pitiful look on his face and told me, "Ah what bro?" I told him sorry. He replied with a, "ah ok ok."

Then our class representative came to us. Her name was Reshma and she told, "you should submit the assignment on Monday. I guess you two will be teammates right, ok I will give to our class teacher your names." Then I turned to Karan, "you ok bro with me being team?" I was surprised that Karan was full in sweat and I was like, "what happened bro?" He told me, "nothing bro", by nodding. When Reshma asked are you ok to Karan, he was just like a mad person telling, "yes I'm ok I am perfectly alright who told you that I have a problem." She just nodded her head in despair and left. I looked at him and told, "bro you should have some courage bro come on bro be a man." I just pity him like anything. He told me, "ok bro we will both get our girls any way possible and we are becoming best footballers." I just laughed at him "ok bro..!" We both started laughing at each other.

After the classes were over we went to the field to play. But when we approached the field, James our senior was watching us talking to Reshma. I didn't realise at that time he had a crush on her and they used to talk a lot. He came to us fuming and told us, "hey useless come here why did you come here?"

And I replied, "bro we want to tell." He just told me, "how

the hell did I become bro to you and call me captain ok?" I said, "sorry captain, I came to play game." He just told me, "ok tell me the rules and tell me at least ten players in under 20 second I will allow you to play."

But I failed miserably. He made us look ashamed in front of everyone at the pitch and we just stayed like useless. Then he told, "whenever you learn all the rules and at least ten football players name you can enter the pitch." We were booed out of the field. But I was not bothered with booing of others. I was only worried about one person because he was with Arundathi when he made a fool out of me. That was unforgivable for me. I felt myself disappointed for the first time in my life. I just turned to Karan and told that we were going to learn football and everything related to it at any cost and that he was coming along with me. He turned to me and told, "why should I come bro?"

"Ok if you are not interested you can leave me bro." He suddenly rushed to me and told me, "whether you are there I am always there with you in everything."

"Ok then come to my house at sharp 9.00 AM tomorrow."

"We had a lot of work to do.9.00 AM bro its too early for Sunday right."

"Then u don't come", and I rushed to my father and he told me, "okk bro your wish. Just call me at least 4 times after 7.00. I'm ok I will not wake up if you didn't call me." And I told him I will do it. I went to father with an angry face and he asked me, "what happened to you?" I never kept anything from my father I told him everything that happened. He replied that they are from a very high family don't quarrel with him. I asked him that I will not quarrel with him but I will prove my talent. I asked my father to stop at a sports shop and asked my father to buy me a football ball. He asked, "why did you need now?" I insisted him to buy me football. I remember that a black one was my first football that cost me around 300 rupees during a 2004 time. When my mother saw football for the first time she asked to me, "you were going to play this my son?" My father told her, "he is in angry mood and let's leave him like that for today."

I just went straight to the tv and turned on the channel in which I first saw my idol. I turned on the tv and it was a news telling that he was wearing a red shirt which a few days before he played against. I just listened to whole session as it was a discussion about his lifestyle and playing style in the channel. I was very curious that even I didn't felt that it was 12.00PM midnight. I was also writing some points relevant to football. My mom called father and showed what I was doing and he told my mom that I remember that it was during a few years ago. He was interested in a sprint competition and he just literally aced it. I wonder what are the things that will be happening to him.

I was so immersed that I just literally looked at every channel and just became more close to my idol. I learned more and more about his life and the things he had to do to get there. I literally felt like relieving his life in mine. I became more immersed in my life. Me and Karan started to practice each day for 2 hours and Sunday for about 4 hours each while learning different formations, different tactics game style, different positions and of course every rules and about 10 footballers I could say 10 footballers in less than 10 seconds. We just literally aced it and I developed various skills and strength and as Cristiano was becoming very skilful and popular on the big stage. I was preparing in a small yard inside my house with my friend Karan. I was very proud that not only I was being a good footballer, I was also transforming Karan into a brilliant goal keeper. I couldn't believe the reflex he had in his body. And my skills were just developing. But the thoughts of Arundathi had never left during my one and a half year time but the thoughts about her just kept me stronger and stronger to do exercise and practice my skills and I was never tired after thinking of her. And after training I told Karan that I just felt like seeing her. He replied to me, "excellent bro even I wanted to see Reshma." "bro I just told and I was taking a nap after exercise." While I was taking some nap after exercise in my yard. Karan came rushing to me and told that you should come and see who is in the front of my house. I told, "I don't care who is it?"

"Hey come on bro!" Karan just tell me making his voice low, "Arundathi bro."

"Wtf man just let me sleep for a little time don't tell me lies bro."

"Hey come on yaar! Just look at your back."

I was surprised at seeing her that I forgot to even find my shirt. I was so immersed in her eyes. She just threw a shirt at my body and tell me, "come on skillzy boy cover your sexy body." I just cover my body suddenly with shirt. Karan told me to just talk something with her and he will be back with something to drink for us. I tried to behave normally and started to take the ball and started practicing. She turned to me and told, "nice game by the way. Did u guys build this?" I nodded and said yes. She then clears throat and tell me, "its been one and half years, where were you not even a word to me. I know its because of James". I told Arundathi to skip the topic. Then she went suddenly quiet and to cheer her up I asked, "why are you here?" She made a laughter face and told me, "hello this is not only your house its also my father's assistant's house and my uncle's house. I can come anytime right uncle?" My father told, "yes daughter you can come anytime. Don't mind him he is like that only."

"By the way I don't come here not only to see uncle but also to tell you that a new coach is coming in our school. And there is an audition for football team I think you and Karan should try for audition." I just nodded at her and she left and I just suddenly started looking at her while she left as she was like an angel. Then suddenly Karan came to my front and just kept the drinks and told me, "have you lost your mind? This was the perfect time to make friends with her and you just lost it."

"I told him that remember our promise only after when we show our talents we will confess our love."

"Bro I think we have watched almost every videos of all coaching instruction in the world and mastered every skill what is left bro. We will go straight to him and make a challenge."

I told him, "yes she only came to tell that there is a football audition for our college team as a new coach is coming." Karan told me, "great news bro. Oh at last I am coming to have a go at my Reshma. How bro you are this much calm while you are not seeing her?"

"Do I look like calm in front of her I didn't looked at her while she was talking to me because not only I was afraid but I feared that I couldn't control my excitement. I think its better to leave her for some time, there is some other priority to me now. And only its football, football and football." Karan hi-fied me and told me that we are going to ace that audition on Monday.

In my mind I always felt this was going to be a very smooth afterwards but sometimes we have to face the life as it should be. We were both prepared for taking our next step in our life. And finally the day had came to of the audition. The players were assigned according to different position. I opted for Striker position which is naturally my idol's position only. But I never had a pleasant feeling in my mind even though I was prepared for every challenge. And then I saw James was coming along with Arundathi and his dad. I found it very difficult to concentrate on the match. But the thing which made me worse was James fuming at me when he looked at me. He suddenly came to me and told, "hey loser! You again this time try to fail miserably." As I didn't know even the audition for captain was already fixed. I was literally fuming at him and told him that I didn't know that the vacancy for the position was fixed for cash. He hold my shirt and told me, "I dare to say the words you just tell." But I was dared to tell the words one more time without even a fear. And I told him, "if you dare beat me one time and your captaincy will be gone boom…His friends hold him back. And I saw he was talking to coach regarding disqualifying me. I thought that this was the end. But the 3 coaches had to agree to make you disqualify but luckily the 3rd coach didn't agree and I was admitted for the trial. Then James came to me and said, "hey loser don't feel too much confidence I know you will loose you piece of shit. You will not even get a chance to speak with Arundathi again I dare you to speak with her." I felt the confidence leave me but I knew that for every Ronaldo fan one thing will cheer him, his famous breath release before every match and free kick. I just did a brief breath release before the audition and it was just perfect for me the audition. There was not even a single mistake and I knew I could ace at everything. As expected Karan with his cat reflexes did just perfect in his audition. Even though James was surprised at our audition he tried to pity us while walking away from the ground. It was very clear that when we left the ground that we knew that we would be selected and it was a great feeling to stand there thinking that last time we felt the booing and now we are feeling the applause of the whole crowd. And the most unexpected thing was that Reshma was watching Karan's game and he was just watching the applauding Reshma and I was happy for him. But I could never apprehend Arundathi because something was not even complete in my life. We just walked out of the ground like champions for the first time I got the taste of glory. And we were waiting for the result to come out. And at last the notice board was filled with audiences and there was great clap in James side as he was again Captain and the main striker. We rushed to see our names and Karan came out telling that he was chosen as 2nd choice Goal Keeper. When I asked what about me he was just telling me, "you….."

"Come on Karan, its ok if I didn't get selected but just tell me."

He suddenly burst into laughter and told me, "you fool! Who told about not making the list you just literally aced the forward position list you are the first choice player with a clear score of 94 percent. Only thing I was sad is that James was our team captain."

I just told him that we can't change everything in our life. Now I told him, "bro you are free to go and make Reshma yours bro." He told me, "sorry bro I forgot to tell you she already told yes to me." I said, "what when bro?"

He told me, "after the selection process I straight went to her and told that I loved her and she without hesitation accepted me."

I was like, "you restless bastard congrats man so happy for

you." Karan turned to me and told, "thanking you for doing a magic in my life and I can never leave you bro in your football I am always with you forever." We embraced each other and I told, "no bro I think you have a new person to care you should be with her."

Suddenly Reshma came to me and told, "no Arun, I think he should be with you, From the moment I saw him I liked him but only one thing that kept me from saying I like him was that he didn't had any aim in his life. I want him to stay like that all the way in his life."

She thanked me for making him like this. I told her that he was always like that but all he needed was just a little push. "Is that right bro?" Karan replied, "yes yes bro." Naturally we all laughed together. Suddenly Reshma told, "I know you like Arundathi, just tell her that Arun." I replied, "thank you Reshma but she is something special and I am not and I am not even in her status, I had to prove something to her." Reshma was about to say, "But Arun… "

I suddenly left for home. Karan told Reshma, "never try to change him, he is always like that. He always likes to give a fight for everything. It's typical Arun."

While I was returning home I was happy for every reason that I was officially allowed to enter the field and no one can stop me and was happy for Karan. But I was confused about one thing, when should I confess my feelings for her……

III
From a die hard fan to pleasure and worries in field

It was the first day of field experience and I was waiting for the exciting coaching sessions from the coach. Suddenly something shocking was seen. Coach came along with James who was our captain. Coach started briefing and tell that for every team, the main player is the captain and he decides everything that happens in the team and so we start the session with the drill session and James will take over from here. I suddenly asked coach,p "sir what is this how can you give someone who is the captain to pick the team players when he has never seen players play?" Coach suddenly turned to me and said, "who is this young man? How much years did you play in pitch?" I said I don't have any field experience. "So I am the coach I decide the things that happen here. So James will pick the team and he will do things properly. If you have any objection you can leave the team is that ok young men?" I was again forced to say yes with me fuming inside me. After coach left us, James divided the groups and held me and said, "hey loser, you tried to act smart you will always run 20 rounds and only after that you will play in my field. Or in the case after you finished your 20 rounds make yourselves better at defending and even after finished that you can get a chance to shoot at goals."

He mocked me and smiled and told, "you only have two hours to come to have at least a go at a goal." I started running around the ground with the despair and sadness in my mind. How much I suffered to get to the place where I am. And I still didn't get the chance to touch the ball and go at the goal. I was devastated and at the end of the training I was barely able to stand up to kick the ball. James saw that and told me, "hey you loser, can't stand up or what? You couldn't even stand up after a short drill . Karan helped me to walk up to my father. He asked me, "what happened son?" I was angry that I couldn't answer to his question. I entered the car and just lie down at the back seat. Karan explained everything to my father. When we reached home, my dad just lifted me from the car and helped me to get back to my bed and my sister was there after coming from college. She saw me and my mother and she asked my father what happened to me and my father told, "let him take rest and we can talk." And father make me take rest at my bed. I woke up at around 10 pm at night. My mother, sister and dad were there all around me and they were waiting to have food along side me. My mom prepared my favourite food for me and dad just helped me to get to my foot. I told father that I will not go to play football and he just lift his hands at my shoulder and told me, "son, I have never seen you passionate about something. You should follow what your mind wish. I am not only telling that even your sister and mother even told me this." I told them that I don't know whether I could last for a week in that camp. That James will make me quit. My dad told me, "the only reason James is doing this because he fears that you will overtake him and you have talent just don't give up your talent for some fellow. Just like the famous Ronaldo's dad can I bet you for becoming the best striker in the world?"

Those words made me cry I just hold my dad and told, "you are the best and you will always be." And my mother and sister asked, "what about us Arun?" "You are 2nd best behind my dad." My sister mocked me and told that, "oh daddy 's son!"

I was going to sleep after dinner and I heard my mother talking to my father, "how will he cope with these rich kids?" He replied, "you know that when he was born he always fought to become best. I know he will become best whoever will stand in his way he will become best." I don't know these words really gave me the boost that I needed.

Its always been my dream to become a good footballer at any cost nobody gets in way. I started my next week training in a calm way because I knew that starting training in a rough way will not help me improve, it will only worsen my condition. So I decided to take training sessions as a part. Like improving sessions one by one, I tried to set a time for 20 rounds running and tried to finish with a better time. These intense training made me only better and better. I got more of a stamina and speed boost and James was planning to introduce me in defense sessions because he never want me to go at a striker position. But even though he tried many ways to stop me he could not do anything to stop my training and he was disturbed at the hard work and intensified training. And Karan was also improving his skills and was turning out to be a great goal keeper. But often in every match I find myself in bench. But I think this hard work and intensity really paid off as there was only one player who didn't like me rest of the people adored me. But James and his particular friends would never accept me as a footballer because in football, there is a particular trend, if we did not praise the captain and started objecting the captain in every relevant matter and the selection process is like not based on stamina level and fitness level. These criteria is just a myth in some teams. Even a player who is drinking alcohol and smoking are getting in front of me as match fit, I could just stand there watching these useless shit who was tired just after 5 minutes of match and they lost their stamina and passes were bad as shit. But they could get in the team every time because of only one thing, because they were like slaves to the captain. I could just only smile at these tactics. And the day came and we were reaching our end of the elementary education and it was our last tournament. I was very happy that James has left the school and there was no chance of him appearing in the team again. And again destiny had other plans. The coach was coming along with James other day. We all were thinking how he could play in the team and yes the solution to the this was announced by the coach himself. As he was our junior faculty player manager and yes this was the end of my life as a football player, I believed that I didn't had a chance to play in the field. And then to my surprise, James came to me and personally told me, "for your team you had to play bro. You are an important part and you will play games trust me, and I want you to be in the best shape." I couldn't believe my ears as he said these words and I just nodded to him like if I was happy. I began my intensified training along with Karan sharpening our every department skills.

And day before match we had a meeting and then James just announced the forward players, I was least bothered about that because even though its my favourite position, I knew that I couldn't play in that position because for a striker there were many experienced players in that position. But my focus was on the attacking wing back and to my surprise he announced that the defense was the same as old team and I couldn't believe that the person with no pace and shit defense how could he replace me. And same was associated with Karan he was replaced by a team favourite, when I told Karan that we should tell this with James he told me, "never mind bro we are in the team right no problem we can get some minutes that's enough or me bro. But I think you just ask about that to James."

I decided to ask James about that and I went and ask him about the team tactics and he explained that I could never leave you because you are just as important player as you are considered as the Super sub. I just nodded at him as I thought he was telling me the most sensible thing for the first time. But at the first 2 matches I didn't even get a single playing minute but I didn't complain to him even I saw that our team players were not even able to walk, James refused to put sub on. And I was like frustrated but I didn't thought that unjustifiable because I believe that team chemistry was important. I was silenced and was in the side-line for the first two match. But during the quarter final match one player was not at all fit at that time. He could not stand up and James was forced to put me and Karan. And for the first time, we got a chance to show our jersey no. 28 and 13 to the world. We felt the most beautiful feeling at that time when the officials announced our name in the mike, "Substitutions 28 Arun and 13 Karan. You might be thinking why should I choose 28 as my number as Ronaldo had no. 7 as the main number. But I believed that the Ronaldo's first number at sporting was 28 and I had ap firm belief that I would wear the first jersey number as same as Ronaldo. And my wish finally came true and I was finally revealed to my first match as a player. I went on to pitch and it was not a nice game. But it was a brilliant game by me. I assist, 7 clearance and 3 tackles. My stats were so impressive that the opposition coach came to me and embraced me and told me to join their team. It was a beautiful day and our names were in the crowd and Reshma and Arundathi were in the crowd cheering our names. But I purposefully never minded Arundathi as I knew that this should deviate my concentration from my game. I had a perfect ovation from the crowd and I came back to my team dugout as a hero. But James just tell a good and changed the subject to next game and he announced, "some players lack fitness and therefore we will be placing Karan and Arun in the starting line up." And we were very happy to know that and I was overjoyed and James told me to be in a good shape for the match. I was in complete concentration for my full debut. I was nervous for my full debut therefore there were a few flaws but it was not my natural position as I was forced to play little defensive but after a few minutes, again those brilliant stats came. No one could dribble past me and I was like a brick wall in the right side. And many times I was fuming to move on the flank like a rocket but I was stopped many times by James himself even though we were 3-1 leading. I was little disappointed but didn't felt ashamed at all because it was my first full game. And day after tomorrow was my first final and I was ready to prepare for that. We were celebrating our first final entry. Karan came and told that Arundathi was waiting for me. I was like, "yes I'm coming", and then James suddenly came to me and told, "hey loser, your time at the pitch is over and we are replacing you with someone with previous reputation and we don't even want you in the substitution bench. You can leave." I was like, "why James?" He told me, "you believe me, a justified and truthful captain to you I will not allow you to taste glory. Glory is for my team you are not even in my team and get out."

I was just at loss for words and I felt crumbled and I was

walking home and Arundathi came to me and asked, "where were you? I was searching for you." I told her, "I am not quite well I just want some free time Arundathi." She told me, "I will tell something that will cheer you up. Reshma told me that you were having a big crush on me and what was that you were imagining me and training, really then why didn't you tell me Arun?" I replied, "what about it?" She replied, "what about it ahhh? You fool I just told you that I like you and you are like what, I just waited for how many days that you would come and tell me I like you and then you were like I should prove her ahh. Arun I fell in love yoy when I saw you as a kid when you was with your father in childhood itself and I started knowing everything about you and I even saw everything the way you looked at me at the class for the first time, and even when I came to your house to see you and you were looking at me when I left from house. Enough of cat and mouse play." She hugged me as Karan and Reshma came in and they told, "love birds need some space ahhh." I was happy at first and wanted to hug her but I saw James look and have a laugh at me. I separated her from me and asked, "did u just tell this to James?" She replied that yes to move away from me. I was so angry that I started clapping my hands at her and told her, "bravo Arundathi, I wonder! Thanks for ruining my life, now please move away from me I should go home."

Karan came to me and told, "what the hell bro? What are you saying? You always wanted this all the time." I replied, "not any more bro.."

I came to my home devastated and it was almost 6 months for the exam and I had to prepare something for the exam. I was focused on studying and Karan came to my house and told me that they won the game and I told, "never mind bro they only wanted me as an object and at the main match we were kicked outside of field. Never mind bro I never want to return to football."

Karan before leaving told me, "Arundathi was crying like anything bro, please talk to her."

I replied, "she only made me lose my spot, I never want to see her again."

"Are you sure bro?", Karan asked me.

I cried and told, "I don't know bro I missed her so much.. but give me some time to adjust bro." Karan told, "ok bro take your time bro but remember one thing bro, she can't hate you she will always love you."

I replied, "I know that bro….I know…."

It was a long exam time and I had to prepare like anything for my exam because my aim was to get a sports college at least according to academics. And exams were over and it was a silent nine months for me and I was preparing to go to a college. And my father came to me and told, "you got admission son, in your favourite arts college where you can also pursue you sports and your academics."

My mind deep down needed a sports college but in my mind I knew that my father's health was not well and my mother was about to get retired, the sister's marriage was coming and I hope to finish my college as fast as I could without taking my parents' help and that's why I opted for a scholarship at every college and my father replied that I got admission in his boss's college and I was like, "why dad why did you make me join there how many months salary have been cut from you as a donation?"

"What son? You got it as a scholarship itself look at the list you are top at that college and you are studying for free. Rest of the college you have to pay a small fees, but if you didn't like the college we can change that, no problem. It's only a small amount in every college. It will not be 20 percent of my monthly income to study at another college."

I replied, "no dad, I don't want to make you pay for my studies." He replied, "ok son, we will get you admission in that college itself and Arundathi is also in that college. Be friends with her ok because she is new to a college atmosphere. Take good care of her she always ask me about you, be with her."

I nodded Yes to my father and he left. Deep in my mind I missed Arundathi like anything but some part of my mind always wanted to move away from her. I don't know what choice should I make, choose her or.. I really don't know. I was sitting in the sofa and was thinking of that. And that was the time when CR7 first won his Ballon d'Or and we were having a blast. Me and Karan were really enjoying it by giving sweets to everyone. Even though football became far away from me I couldn't get out of this fantasy world and especially not a chance to miss my idol's game…….

IV
The spotter of a great talent

And yes the long awaited first day of my college came, but I was not at all expecting some changes that will happen around me. The things which made me happy was around me. Karan was there with me all the time and I had Arundathi at a hand's distance from me, even though my mind never allowed me to talk to her.

Yes, the first day of my college life came, me and Karan were ready to face a new hostel life. But the smooth and nice day was turning to a bad one as James was again waiting for me there. And the bad thing was that he was the senior in the same college and the best feeling soon turned to a nightmare. But I always think we had to move on. As soon as James saw me he called me close for ragging and there was Arundathi along with him. I thought this was again going to be a bad life time. But the luck was again about to turn right to me. When one big person came close to me and said, "Arun, its Arun right? Remember me? The coach of the team you faced at school level, Roshan." I suddenly remembered him and told him, "Yes coach I remember you."

And he told me that he was the new temporary faculty in this college as the sports coach. Again he admired my playing style and he insisted me in coming to field. But I refused and he asked me, "what's the problem, Arun?" I told, "nothing coach." And he saw me moving away from James. He called

James and told him, "James you will never rag him or will remove him from field. If you do that son, your captaincy and player status will be stripped and trust me son when I tell you will be stripped. You will never enter pitch again, while I am in charge." James with a bitter face accepted it. And coach told me to change the room close to my room. I was just relieved. And when I began walking I heard Arundathi was waving at me, But I didn't bother to mind her. She was calling me, "Arun.."

But all my focus was on one thing again, which was on playing football and reaching heights again as both Karan and me started preparing again. And I believed that coach had something extraordinary in him and he will bring the better in both of us. It was again a beautiful day for me at the football pitch as the training schedule was entirely new for me. As coach came and introduced me to all the team and almost everyone accepted me as a player and James and some of his friends only had a bitter feeling about it. But the coaching session was entirely new to me. It was not at all about practical experiences only but it was about learning football about theoretical aspect. Like coach was telling about different styles of football we had to use again different type of opposition and sudden responses that a player should possess while on the pitch and about transforming small changes in position without having major changes in football. And it was coach who explained to all of us and tell James who obviously is the captain in our team to explain his view. I felt extremely well in his technique because I believe he was transforming us into intellectual and disciplined footballers rather than an unknown, raw footballers. And at the end of the session he was asking to explain the tactics of 4-4-2 formation and coach called James to illustrate different ways of arranging formation. Because one thing he hated was to be taught by someone else and the most irritating thing was that he didn't care for the game or discipline and he never used to watch the tactical side of football and it was usual as coach will again explain what's behind that. But that day coach looked at me and told, "Arun what do you make of this formation?" James wasted no time in mocking me straightaway, "who the hell is he to explain tactics he didn't even know about rules when I first met him." Coach told James to keep quiet and asked me to tell what I knew. I humbly replied to him, "coach I am not at all experienced at field and I had played only 2 or 3 matches at a club level." He asked me, "Arun whether you know it or not while you were playing against my team in school level one of thing which has happened to me that you guys were playing in 5-3-2 formation and the left back in the formation was drifting forward and the mid fielders were on the two sides covering his wing and I saw that Arun was moving from his right wing back role to a more central defensive mid role." Coach asked James why was he coming to CDM role, James replied, "to attack the lost ball from the left back." Coach said, "brilliant wow total idiotic answer. Arun just tell him why did you do that." I replied, "when our LB lost the ball I saw the space for the striker was open as my right wing back role was covered by central mid field player. The most sensible thing was to close the gap for a pass to striker as the path was clear for attacker as 3 CBs were disoriented and was at different position marking their wing backs and it was a clear shot for striker." Coach replied, "this is what I call a well clear and cool answer. Well done Arun. So you know what's an intellectual play. So just go for it."

I came to the team board and told them, "a 4-4-2 formation can be arranged with 4-2-2-2 or 4-2-2-1-1 as in the first formation we use two attacking midfielders and 2 strikers. And in the latter we will use a second striker for more support and attacking tactics."

Coach applauded me and told, "excellent Arun. This is just the way you should learn the game. So I think today's session is over so go to the field according to position." He instructed Karan to be at the goal keeper position. And I asked Coach if can I join the attacking session and he told me, "Arun, I need to talk to you." He called me and said, "I knew you always dreamt of being an attacker, As I knew that you follow strict principle of Ronaldo lifestyle. But trust me you are versatile. I can put you in different position. So you can practice all session but I think you should practice more in RB and CDM role."

I was literally heart broken and I told him that. "But sir, it was my dream to play as attacker, as a fan, I always dreamt of becoming an attacker just like Ronaldo." Coach told me, "you don't want to remove your idol principle. You just have to make it in a different position. Trust me Arun, you will be the game changer."

At last I was convinced and agreed to train at this position. And under his training session I was becoming more of a complete football player. He made me watch the videos of the great Philip Lahm and told me to adapt his playing style in my game. And during each session I was overtaking James in every session and James was getting frustrated each day. And my football on field experience was getting better and our school principal was visiting one day and Karan and me was watching alongside and we heard that coach was discussing with principal that how good I was and Coach was telling him, "Sir you just have to watch him play. He is just brilliant and sir he will be a great player in Indian team if he keeps his head straight and play." And one thing which surprised me that he asked the principal about making me the captain of the team. I was literally in tears as many memories of being useless and missing finals came to me. I just went away from there, because that was too much for me in a short time. But Principal told that no way we can replace James sir from permanent captaincy. Coach asked "why sir? He is such a partial captain and unprofessional as close it becomes to the game." Principal replied, "we can't change that because his father is a valuable asset to the college and his father is a close friend of our MD. So at most we can make him vice captain." In despair Coach told principal, "this is the most cruellest thing that can happen in football sir." Principal replied, "what can we do coach? Person with the money is always the King."

But none of these captaincy was a matter to me at all. I was so happy to be acknowledged by a great coach as talented. It was really something special for me.

V
The rise of the great talent

The training for the next day was starting and there was a team meeting for players by coach. Coach came and revealed that this was an important meeting and we are going to see our new vice captain and naturally we believed that it was for our main goal keeper who is the friend of James. They were almost celebrating like anything and suddenly coach pointed the finger at me and told that I was our vice captain and this announcement was shell shocking for James and me. James just shouted at sir, "what the hell coach you always complained of being partial to me, what are you doing now?"

"If there is any problem James you can tell me calmly. And for god's sake this is not your team. If you want to stay and play, obey me."

"For f*** sake I'm not playing in this team", James fumed and moved out of the ground. Coach cleared his throat at the silent environment and told, "So, it's clear now Arun will be our captain and Jacky you will be the vice captain. If any one of you has any doubt you can ask me." Coach dispersed us for training but I stayed there and said, "coach I am too young to take this position."

Coach replied, "there is no young or old in the captaincy. It all depends upon understanding the game and usually this is attained by experienced players but you already have attained it at a young age. So don't worry about it. Trust me Arun, you are a special player and will always be remembered."

I was moving out to field and I just turned to him and said, "thanks coach for believing in me I won't let you down." He replied, "I know that Arun will you just go and practice?"

I smiled and said, "yes coach.. I am going."

In my mind I was just living the most beautiful time of my life. Everything was there for me, the freedom, I wish to play in my position and the team was having a great chemistry and me and Karan was having the time of our lives. My captaincy was becoming a talking point in my college. Everyone was talking about it. But we had an important intercollege competition approaching where this was the most important competition to me as a player and captain. I was practicing very hard for the match and I saw Arundathi was watching my practice and coach saw me and Arundathi looking at each other. Coach went to Arundathi but she didn't see coach. Coach asked her, "what are you looking for?" She replied, "nothing coach, I was just......"

Coach replied, "yes you were just watching. Look I know you people have fantasies about great players, please he is not a person to waste your time, there is lot of time to waste with some other people."

Karan came in between the conversation and told the whole story to coach. Coach after hearing the story told Arundathi, "No problem beta, we will deal with it."

While I was returning from the pitch, coach called me and asked, "Did you know some Arundathi? I was saying like, "coach....

He replied to me, "yes I know who she is. The girl you love and she loves you back. But what the hell Arun? You believe that it's all because of her that you didn't play the final. She was the sole reason for you to pick football. No wonder you lack confidence in the pitch. You are carrying a big load in your heart. Arun she is here just tell her what you feel because it's big time you tell her that you love her."

Coach left and Arundathi was standing in front of me and I was about to tell Arundathi that I'm sorry and she suddenly started hitting me. "What did you tell me you waste of time ah?" She was pushing me and I held her hand and embraced her and told her that I'm sorry I am never leaving her again. She just look up to me and asked, "are you not saying that you love me?"

I replied, "how much time you want to hear I love you?" "I only want to hear one time but you have to hug me until I tell you to stop."

I smiled and look at her and said ok. It was again nice time for us. I really enjoyed the time with Arundathi, Karan and Reshma and everything was going smoothly and it was all going perfectly. Like everything, I touched victory during that time. And the most important day of my life was coming and it was the night before it. Coach called us for the final team talk before the game and told us the instructions before our last practice match and before going to our practice he took a special gift for me and told me to open it and it was a band with captain written inside it and he told me to wear it and told me, "Arun, I know you are a great captain. You will be the most perfect captain. Never feel doubtful in taking a decision." I nodded at him and he told me to wear that captain band in my arm. I told to coach, "you gave me this position and I think you are the best person to make me wear that." Coach took the band and placed it on my arm and all the team mates were applauding. I think that will be the most memorable moment in my life. And with the captain arm band I was feeling lot confidence and was feeling responsible and while I was walking to the ground I just looked at the sky and remembered Ronaldo who always has been an inspiration to me. I knew that the time has come for me to do the next step in my life. And it was the match day and everything was sorted. The line up was done and the team talk before the match was going on and coach told me that they are high tackling side and we have to be very careful to avoid injury and try to get every foul possible. And coach said, "come on captain, give your last speech before match." I just closed my eyes and prayed for a second and started my speech, "look guys, I'm new to this field and I don't have a previous experiences in these matches, but the only thing I can tell you is that we all are players we make mistake, we don't try to blame the mistake upon each other. We are a team and if one of us fail every one fail, so if you see someone commit a mistake don't feel ashamed and don't harass him. We are the team. Believe that whoever comes with better belief and great will power will win the match and there is only one team in this field which is better at these that is our team so we are the ones who will win."

The match was about to start and coach came to my ear and whispered, "today is a big day and there are a lot of people here who are great. You show them what you are capable of." I was standing to come out of the field first as in the commentary they were calling the team sheet and the name No. 28 Arun, captain of our college was literally creating a wave in the college and there was Arundathi cheering for me in the crowd. Me and Karan had our fist bump and was about to begin the game after the ceremony. And the game was progressing and Coach was on side-line and a person approached him and talked to him, "any talent in the team, Roshan?" And coach replied, "yes sir there are a few people who you should note, and yes there is a captain material for the Indian team sir."

"Is it?"

Coach replied, "yes sir. Arun, captain of our team sir, you should definitely watch his game." The official replied, "yes Roshan I will take a look at him."

The match was a great match as we were having a great game and our defense was so good that no ball entered the penalty box and we were playing an attacking high line and I was playing the dictating role and the official was really enjoying my style of playing as I was wanting more and more ball all the time and was dictating like a true no. 6. And thanks to that we won the game 1-0. And after the game we were enjoying and suddenly the official came to me and told, "well played boy! You definitely have a good future as a captain and as a CDM perfect positional playing. Keep it up son. A few more good games at this level and a top club will come for you and then it will be straight to Indian team."

His words were like music to me, and we were enjoying the game and Arundathi came to me and told me, "today we will go out." And I asked, "today?" She replied, "yes today and you are coming with me." I at last said, "yes I will come." We were at outside and having fun and the person who I was not meeting for a few days saw me with her. It was James and I saw his vengeance towards me in his eyes. Even though I loved her company I was totally not enjoying it. I reached at night towards coach's room and said, "coach I have seen James and I think he has some vengeance inside him for me. I saw him it his eyes."

Coach replied, "no way Arun he came to see me and told

that he was so sorry for what happened between you and hin and tomorrow he will come and see you and will apologise to you in front of everyone." I replied to him, "ok coach if you trust him I believe you coach." Even though I left from coach's room, I was not at all convinced with his transformation…

VI
The downfall

I was waiting eagerly for next day's training, but there was always some fear in me. And at last James apologised to me in front of everyone and embraced me and he told me in ears, "we will see what happens in your next match", and he smiled at me and I thought that something very dangerous was coming to me and it all started in the training session next day when Karan was injured in a training session which I clearly saw his legs injured. And I was talking very fiercely with James about it, but I usually was very calm. Coach saw this and came and told me while shouting, "this is how a captain handles a situation? You are removed from captaincy Arun. I think after all, experience matter. In some times."

He gave captaincy again to James and I saw that evil laughter in him towards me, I knew everything was going downhill from no own. I tried to convince coach, tell about James and his suspicious behaviour. But coach thought it as a defense for loosing my captaincy. And I knew something was going to go wrong in the semi finals of the competition. And the officials were also watching this competition. Even though while entering the field I suddenly lost my confidence in communication with goal keeper and even the whole defense was shapeless and I tried to point this to coach many times but coach was too submerged under his opinion. He always see the outlay of the field but he never mind to do it because he thought it was my selfish nature of pointing out mistakes of James as my frustration of giving captaincy to James. And before the match was about to start James told me, "this will be your last match and the whole college will you hate for it." He tapped with smile and told me that. When he told that I was not expecting this and the game was really fixed that there was unnecessary marking to leave me in the most vulnerable position for making defense open at me. And I sometimes had to cover up to 3 players at a time. And the biggest vulnerable position was coming as I saw the whole defense was playing on counter and the ball lost to striker and James faked a fall behind me and he looked at me and told me that you are screwed and he was marching towards the goal I was running like bursting out my heart but I couldn't reach him at the time and the striker was through and the goal keeper was in a more advanced position in penalty box. I knew there was almost no time left. And I knew that I had to do it I went for the rough tackle to cover up the defense and I was able to put a stop at striker but I knew what was coming on me and it was a straight red and at the last minute of the game and James was disappointed in not conceding a penalty and a free kick. Almost the whole stadium who praised me started booing me, but I knew that was the most sensible thing to do, even the opposition coach came and told me, "even if you injured a player that was the great professionalism for a team son." He patted my head and back. I was so frustrated in getting a red card, but I knew that something was wrong. He was left footer and I knew his position was just adjusted for the curl to left and I shouted at goal keeper to turn left and keep a more advanced to jump to left but he was not listening to me and James told everyone to cover the right side and the most stupid thing was that even though wall was for right he forced keeper to move more to right and I knew that before he was going to kick I knew that was a goal and after the kick the exact left curl happened and turned to left post and as predicted it resulted in a goal and all the team was in desperate mood to getting knocked out of competition. But I saw James laughing at me. At that time I had only one thing in mind, to thrash James and I was rushing to the field and started a huge fight between us. Coach came between us and pulled us back and I shouted at him, "coach, James was responsible for what happened. He opposed my instruction in field." Coach slapped me and shouted at me, "it was only because of you….we lost your stupid challenge and we lost it and now you turned into a rogue player." He asked me to leave the pitch forever and don't come to this pitch anyway. I couldn't believe what happened to him and in full tears I left the ground where the whole crowd was booing and Karan came to me and told me, "Bro don't mind this crowd, please go home now." I pushed him and told him, "leave me bro…"

I was so desperate that day I straight away went to my dad and I was crying all over in his lap. He calmed me and told me, "look son, I know this is hard and you are about to finish the course but I am getting old and I am not able to continue my job and your mother is retired and I know you never asked any money or anything from me. But for a few years please look after us. Leave this football and look for a proper job. May be this is only for rich people and influential ones."

I nodded at him and said, "yes dad, I will." Suddenly, the Indian team official came to my house and called me. He told me, "I'm sorry to tell you Arun, you are blacklisted by your coach so you can't apply for any standard club for 3 years. I knew what you did in the pitch was sensible. I see that your coach can prohibit you from the field. But he can't ban you from side-line."

I was not able to hear anything after I told I was blacklisted by coach, I asked in tears, "why sir but why did he do it?" "I know Arun, but sometimes coaches don't see the right side of the game. They are blind towards the actual mistakes in the game when they loose. So I know your family background. You need a job so I'm offering you one in my academy and I'm offering you a career also. Join here and tell my name, Michael, and give this document. Your admission will be done. You are given a quarters for you and your family, and there will be a regular salary also." I told him, "thank you for the offer sir, but I need to adjust my life without football." He turned at me, "who told you about quitting football, I am offering you a chance to re-launch it."

I looked at the document and saw that it was a coaching academy football coach. He asked me, "what do you say Arun? Regarding a new beginning at a coaching academy for coaches. I know this is a quick decision and even though you are very young for a coach, I hope that this is something which will suit you more. After a minimum of 7 years, you will be a officially a licenced coach."

I didn't hesitate to say yes to that proposal because being attached to football is something I can't change and still I can live this dream. And he told me, "you have almost twelve hours to join there so I suppose you can leave today itself and let family come tomorrow." I nodded at him and called the most important person in my life and told her that. "Arundathi, I don't know when I will return or will I ever return, I just wanted to tell you before leaving that I love you so much and I will miss you a lot." Arundathi asked where I was going and I told her, "I can't be here in this college while I can't play football and I want something new in my life." She replied to me, "I will be waiting for you…"

Before I disconnected the call I said, "tell Karan that I enquired about him and I will return for you." I disconnected the call and began my travel to a new place, for a new adventure and for a new chapter in my life…………

While I joined the academy, my family was happy and my sister's marriage was over and I was completing all my debts in my life. While learning every new trademark skills in coaching and training by famous professionals made me better at footballing knowledge. It was something refreshing for me and took each sessions at every institute in India, attended almost every conferences and 6 years passed by and the thoughts of my college, Karan and Arundathi never left me. My mind was always wondering when was the right time for a return to my hometown where I can actually hope to get back some glory which I lost. My mind was filled with thoughts and it was almost like a time where I had nothing to do here in the academy and suddenly one day Michael came to me with a Spanish scout and he was telling me that actually he liked my views which I used to conduct the plays and he told me, "whenever we get a vacancy, we will call you."

I was like, "sir seriously? Indian making a chance to coach at somewhere in Spain." We started laughing and he left and Michael told me, "Roshan wanted to see you for a long time and he has been telling me so many times to tell you about this, but I refused because you were having a great time and good performances and I felt like I don't want to ruin it." I told him, "Michael why will I return to him? He told me that I am not good for football and ruined my life and now he want to change all that.?" Michael calmed me and told, "Arun calm down we know that it was all wrong and Roshan couldn't see it and Karan couldn't stand not proving your innocence and he forcefully made him watch the match and coach was convinced but he was late to change his decision and James was placed in Indian Team, by himself by his suggestion and now Roshan is coaching one of the greatest Sports college in India and he is one of the highly paid coach with a full crew." And I told him, "what's the importance for that? It's all over. He enjoyed a great time on field in Football so what's the matter?" Michael told me, "now carefully listen Arun. The college you left had a free post in coach's position."

I replied, "what nonsense sir? It's the place where coach plays." Michael told me, "yes Arun he is leaving as the head coach and there is a position vacant and he wants you to be there. I know you will not be welcomed there but I know victory from there will be something sweet to begin for you and I know Roshan had done something very dumb in his life for you and now its time for him to make that right. Now its all your decision to take the job or not." I asked Michael to give me a few days time to think. Michael nodded and left. In my mind there was lot of things, wondering how will I accommodate and the fear of getting rejected haunted me like anything and whenever I closed my eyes the one thing that came in my vision was all the persons booing around me. And at morning I saw Michael and told him that I am going to my homeland and to inform Coach. Michael replied, "perfect Arun, I will book you air ticket. Be ready by evening. Your flight is at 6:00 PM." I was packing everything for my return trip and all that was left was asking permission from my parents while returning. Dad told me, "you cared for us for a long time and as a son you were perfect to us and I asked you to quit playing and you did it and now I should let you fulfil you aim, otherwise as a father, I will not be able to complete my duty. Goand be happy."

And I travelled back to where it all began and wished at least that time, it would be a happy ending..

VII
After a long break

And the long journey ended at the doorsteps of my Coach. I knocked the door of the person who made me who I am today but was afraid to face him still today. Door opened and I saw a fat and old Roshan Sir. He was very happy to see me and embraced me and was crying holding me. He was telling me that he knew that I will come and coach mocked me by saying that, "you became fat champ", and I laughed at him and he told me to have a seat and he will bring me a cup of tea. And I asked about Coach and his family. He replied that every one was fine and they always enquired about me. We had a discussion about football and as usual about my idol Ronaldo. Even with ages, I couldn't forget his principles, his practices and we were having a great time and I just broke the delightful time and asked him, "coach I want to know that what is my job as a coach?" He told me, "I knew you were going to ask me. You can join from tomorrow onwards and you can see your friend Karan. He is the assistant coach and Arun, one more important thing. This is not the team like old days. It's unprofessional as you don't like it to be."

I replied, "coach I was looking for something to build rather than a well roofed squad. Now I think it should be challenging and interesting and I told him that I am taking his leave and I'm off to meet Karan. Before I left coach told me, "Arun, I know that this post is nothing compared to what I had taken from you, but I can offer this much only." I replied, "I only want one thing coach, your blessings and prayer."

And I left to meet one of the most difficult person to tame, Karan himself. I knew that I will not get a glad welcome from him. I went to his house and saw a kid playing and saw Reshma running after the kid and when Reshma saw me, she came to me and was smiling and told me, "where were you Arun? Where did you go?" I replied that, "where is Karan?" She replied with a grin that he was inside and she told me, "be careful Arun." I told, "relax Reshma I know what to do about it."

I entered the house and heard a bald and fatty person come out and shouting, "Reshma where is my car key?" And he looked at me and stayed stunned for a second and asked me, "who are you?" And he called Reshma, "why did you let strangers in the house. I told him, "am I a stranger to you ah..?" He replied me with a big hockey stick coming to me and was telling me, "don't you dare speak to me. How dare you leave me without telling a word? I am like a stranger to you right? I have been with you as a shadow for almost 8 years and not even a single word to me and I had to hear it from Arundathi." I told him, "sorry bro relax I will make up for that." I told Reshma to make some food as I was very hungry. And it was a great time and Karan told me about Arundathi. "She will be happy to hear that you are around Arun." "I know that Karan", I replied.

So I told him all the story and the situation now. Karan told me, "ok Arun we will start from tomorrow. You should be needing a place to stay, right?" I told him, "I am moving to hostel bro." He told me, "ok. And Arun, its not the same team you had when you left. The whole team is a mess now and we have a lot of things to discuss and we have a lot of work to do."

I replied, "I know bro, we will start the sketch from today onwards. Karan told me, "it's good to be back with you bro. We really missed you." I smiled at him and told him that I want to see Arundathi and Reshma replied, "when I saw you I already called her you don't worry about it." Reshma asked me to get changed you look tired and I nodded and went to changing room to get dressed.

I had a fresh bath and came to have a tea and there was Arundathi with the tea and I was just staring at her beauty for a short time and I just took the tea from her and hold her close to me and she was telling me, "never leave me for anywhere for so long." I just told her I never will do it anyway and she told me, "I really missed you and I replied, "I missed you too, but I had something responsible to do." She nodded and told, "coach told me about that and I do not care how much time you needed to adjust, achieve what your mind says and after that we can settle down once and for all." There was a knock on the door and Karan and Reshma were asking, "is it the right time to come inside?" Me and Arundathi laughed and said, "yeah please…"

Karan came and I told him, "bro, get ready we have to visit some places, make arrangements." He asked, "so where is it?" I told him, "to the place where our football journey began." Karan was like, "straight to college so early?" I nodded at him like, "nah to our first training ground, our home, my home…"

VIII
Revisiting fields

It has been some time since I last visited my home, my real home. To my surprise there was nothing much of a change rather than the dust left by our training facilities and those sort of stuffs. Karan was telling me each and everything, the training methods, the mode of exercises. As he reminded all the things for me, every memory was even fresher. After a brief gap of exposure to our nostalgic memories, we were back to the coaching staff set up. I asked him, "how many coaches are there in the club and he laughed and told me, "bro, we are only the two guys that are left in coaching and the whole bunch of lazy buffoons." I told Karan, "it's not the time to joke. We have to set up the whole coaching team." And I started to assign a list of who were working in the college having interest in sports and those who had previous experiences. Main ones we were lacking was a midfield and an attacking coach and at last, with the help of coach Roshan, we were able to convince the coach team to come to a conclusion. To my luck, there were still people who were devoted at this age to football. So the whole coaching team was set up and our first meeting was set up and the only one thing that came to my mind in the session was the whole bunch of coaches were requested by me to start the training earlier. There were still 3 days to join my post so I decided to send them to watch my team while I watch my team far from the distance. And I used to walk at some distance and observe the players. One thing that I noticed about the players was complete lack of professionalism but still there were exceptions. Once I saw a player who was training alone and I asked him, "why are you not playing?" He replied, "I am used to sitting on bench and never expected to start a game." I asked his name he replied to me his name was Krishna and I asked him, "Krishna, let's go out to play at that part. I guess you are not so busy." He replied, "I am ready." I just checked his passing range by asking him to put a long ball and he just surprised me and he delivered a full straight lofted pass with a slight curve. It made me curious and asked him to make a shot for the gap between the trees. To my surprise that was an excellent long shot and with various training he showed me that he is a good crosser of the ball and I just wanted to check his defensive attribute because I realised that he was not showing any weakness in stamina and I see him as a more efficient runner of the pitch. I asked him to defend me and just as I passed, he went to dribble a double tap. He put a Rabona style tackle and I was amazed to see that and I asked him, "how did you do it?" He told me, "this is a style I developed myself while playing." I asked him that he knew any players who could do this like you and he told me that there were bunch of people who never used to play there but they have talent and asked that which all positions do they play. He replied me that there were 3 players, one is a person who is very much a dictator of the ball. He used to defend his ball and make the ball moving because of his strong physique. And one person is a striker who could get a shot from any position around the box like he is a goal poacher. And another person is someone who can run down the wings and I asked him to bring these players anyhow tomorrow. And before leaving I asked him, "which position do you play?" "I like all the positions. I like to run down the field."

I told him, "ok and we will see you tomorrow." And at night I asked Karan about Krishna and he told me that Krishna is just a short tempered person and he is never disciplined on the pitch. I asked him, "who is disciplined and who is not bro? I have seen this boy and I know what he can do to our team. He is a very broad minded player who could bring different variety of styles to the team." Karan told me, "bro let me put him in the team tomorrow itself. Wait I had to look at a few players also I will give you the final team tomorrow morning." Just as the previous evening I saw Krishna but today he was accompanied by 3 friends and he asked me like, "we don't have much time." I don't know how I bring them. "So let's play a short game", I told him and I asked the 3 persons about the positions they play and I was convinced and I put a team to test their abilities and after the game I came to knew that they had the intelligence but one thing that they lack was on field positioning and game time. At the end of the game they asked who am I and what's my job. I pretended like that I am a club trainer and I asked them to come tomorrow and said, "I will come with our chief coach and we will see can you 3 can make the team." They were very happy and asked me that where should they come and play and I replied, "this ground". They told me that the main team is playing there. I replied to them, "we will see you guys come tomorrow at this ground."

Me and Karan went on a long discussion along with other coaches and I asked them, "There are five players who are not fit to the team. Then why you guys are training them like first team players." They told me that they were very vastly experienced and they could offer our team a lot and I replied them, "yes they can offer us a lot of fatigue and tiredness. Like did you see how they run? They can't even run ten rounds and how will they defend against these pacy sides. No wonder there were major fails during last year. All I am saying is that don't remove them from the team. Of course they matter to our team but they are just utility and circumstantial players so we had to use them according to that only. So we are building a new team." After the meeting was dispersed I told Karan, "there are still people like us man. Like how can this happen bro?"

"Before you came it was just me and these bunch of players. How can I manage these players bro? So even management are a lot tougher in giving funds and with you only now the current coaches were convinced to join and I never had a thought about the rest of the players." I told him, "don't worry man, we will change this." The next morning had come and now it was the day that for the first time in my life I am going to become a coach and there was sort of a pressure down to my shoulder, but moreover I really enjoyed that mind and profession in developing players and how to take them to an elite level. When I dressed up and came out, Karan told me, "bro you look really good today. Let's bring this team your passion, energy and hunger for victories." And when I was moving to the ground I saw Krishna along with his 3 buds and they were looking in sort of a puzzled way at me. Karan asked for a team regrouping and I told Karan to bring Krishna and the 3 boys here. At last the team was regrouped with all the players along with Krishna. That was my first time as a coach for a pep talk and I was too nervous and a bit worried about me but somehow I managed to find my seriousness. I shouted, "Boys I am your new chief coach", and I could see Krishna's face was literally filled with surprise. "As you know, for me this is my first experience as a coach so we are both learners of this game but here only I have one thing that I would like to learn from you guys, how to be a better footballer. As a player just show me because I have never been to a top level player but the only thing I can guarantee is that I have been in the side-lines for various games and seen the team victorious with my tactics. So I don't measure a player purely based on talent. Talent is worthless unless you don't have the hard work. So my training will be purely based on intensity and hard work and if you have a problem with that I guarantee you that you will never be picked in my team. I don't believe in having a talented player as show off. One other thing I will specify is that you cannot bunk your classes or have your grades down because of training. After all education is also part among the age group of your people. Regarding the game part, as I have mentioned before, the team will be picked only on the basis of your training performances. So I want you to be up to the level in training. And training starts at morning 5 A.M - 6 A.M, which will be focused on the physical aspects of the game mostly and evening 4 – 7 PM will be training session and in a month you will have some football learnings also. In most trainings they don't use it because they don't believe to increase the football intelligence. For me, my team should be able to make decisions even if without my presence at the ground. I can only guide you. You have to make the decision. So let me introduce you to your three new team mates." I introduce Krishna and his friends to the team. I could see that happiness in their faces, the first laughter of appreciation and I believe that's the important thing a player requires at any time during his career. Then I asked Karan to conduct our first training session which begins with a warm up and I was observing their gameplays. As my expectation, Krishna was doing fantastically but there were some of the players I could feel that their lack of sportsmanship is affecting the game. But despite that, one player suddenly caught my eye other than Krishna. It was John in whom I saw another brilliant attacking midfielder. But I saw his company was a little bit of oddness. But he was a silent stick to his behaviour, disciplined player who can control his game on his own. Perfect example for a creative midfielder. The defense and goal keeping department was well with experienced players so my only concern was injury and stamina issues and therefore I know and believed that I could find alternatives for them also. In forwards, the new recruits were showing excellent awareness and positioning and I was even less worried about that because the new recruits were perfectly blended with the experienced hands and I know that we have stars in every corner of the team. One of the main thing that is necessary in controlling a game is none other than team chemistry which is obtained by complimenting each other. And after all, that was again in trouble due to one player. Raghu, who is the team captain, he is the perfect example for a non disciplined player. He got the talent but drugs, smoking has ruined him and he has no future as he is clearly showing deterioration and along with this he is a parasite who is disturbing the team who needs to be removed and John, who is the major companion of him and ruining him is my main problem. I didn't know how to remove this bugs from a good team without altering the chemistry. My mind was always puzzled. At last the situation and performances were going deep down due to his involvement so I had to make a drastic decision which caused another problem.

IX

A needed change

One day, I announced the team for a practice match with Raghu and his team on the bench. Suddenly, Raghu raised the voice, "coach what the hell did I do to sub me off?" I told him, "you were never fit for this whole training days. How will I trust you to do well in the match? So you are on the bench. Prove your fitness, I will make you a regular player and for god's sake I saw how much tired you were after completing one round." He suddenly raised at me and said, "but I am the goddamn captain, coach." I told him, "you were, not today, on my watch." So he shouted at me, "ok Mr. Perfect, who is the new captain?"

I said, "there will be two captains. I haven't decided who will be vice and main. Krishna and John will be your captains." I then turned to Raghu and told him, "if you want to play, stay by my rule or you can leave." He then turned to me and told, "who the hell are you to coach me? You are nothing. I am leaving here, we will see who is the better footballer."

I replied, "I bet there is only one winner here, that is me." He accompanied his two nuisance players and left. I was happy with their to leave my team but John was a big factor for me and I was worried that this could affect the game but I have to do it for the good nature of the game. John was rushing to stop Raghu and Raghu replied, "John, come with me. He is not a good player. At his time, he left this college with a big failure

59

on his head. You don't need to be coached by this shit." John replied, "I can't leave this team because of my father. I don't want to land him in trouble. Already he has been suffering because of me." Raghu replied, "but never play for him with your talent. This team doesn't require you. See coach only gave Krishna's name first because he knew he has to kick you out somehow so you will be eventually kicked out and Krishna might be the shrewd mind behind it. Trust me bro, I will be waiting for you. Let's chill and there are many teams waiting for me. I will find one for you." He replied, "I felt that too Raghu. Without you it will also be difficult for me. But trust me I won't play any better for this team. I will play for me." Raghu smiled and said, "yeah man, that's it. Will see you in the evening." I knew that this was going to be a lot tougher, to change him from Raghu's influence and I knew one thing, without him our team will definitely lose.

And yet again our training sessions were beginning and I found out from Krishna that there were a lot of good players who refused to play in field but have different qualities around them. So I put a request to college management regarding the post for hostel warden in order to spot out talent. To my luck, I was blessed to have so many team players there and my biggest concern of complimenting the team was solved as each of my issues were getting solved from one end. It was starting on from other end and I was about to face a big loss of chemistry in the midfield between Krishna and John, who I believed to be the key players of the team. The performances of John without Krishna was simply brilliant and with Krishna, it was my worst fear on the field. I thought gradually with time, it would fade away but these issues were very much highlighted in the game and the time came to solve the issues between them. Because this was about to become real personal in life.

X
A Big time coming

Yes, the training session was going quite well and the only worrying factor in the field was Krishna and John. It was the day Coach Roshan was visiting me and told me, "Arun, why didn't you continue the game after the blacklist ban was lifted?" I replied, "coach, I always wanted to come back to the field but after three years of blacklisting and embarrassments, I returned to field but I was no longer able to feel that happiness I had during my practice time at those days. It was long gone and I don't want to make my family unhappy because my family was a lot dependent on me so I had to take up coaching course and with Michael's help, I was able to join an academy as coaching staff and managed some small academies and somehow I was able to manage my family and after sister's marriage, parents were happy and there were no difficulties for them. So I had my mind set to return. Then arrived your call so I got back." Coach looked at me and said, "it was my life's biggest mistake to blacklist you and I hope that god gave me one chance to correct that." I told coach, "no need coach. You taught me everything. I am very much thankful to you for your service and that is past coach, leave it." He replied, "yeah, leave it." He asked, "what is your stand on Arundathi?" He told me to approach her father regarding this. "And I remember Arun, during your playing time, you cared for her without giving much attention because you were always afraid that you were inferior

61

to her regarding money but you have one thing that their whole family lacked Arun, the talent and vision, you have both, you will reach the top." I told him, "coach, her father already knew this and you know he already told her that he will never accept someone who is not having a constant job or stability and he is planning a marriage with James also, I don't know how much time I can fight for her." Coach looked at me and told, "anyway, leave it Arun. There is an important competition coming and I wish you should participate in it because the best manager in the game will get a chance to coach team India but there will be many leading clubs also participating, along with sports college. So as Arundhati's father has sold the college, you will be more free to approach the management regarding sponsors and I have talked about it to chairman and he is happy for the team to participate there and moreover your results are impressive according to his views and Michael was also telling me that you were in the eyes of Indian FA, so this is your chance." I replied, "I will participate coach, for sure but you know that James is coaching in of the biggest clubs in India so you know my chances are very slim. It's not because I don't believe in my talent because money is always above talent here coach." He replied, "but this time I am telling you will win this. Rest, leave it to me and Michael. We will handle it. Consider this as my apology for my mistake."

With the belief that this is my last chance to get something achieved in my life, I had to win this at any cost and the next thing that happened made me obsessed with this. For registration of competition I went with Michael to FA. There, I saw my biggest enemy James who was coming for registration also and stopped by me and told, "what's up, loser? What brings you here? Looking for stadium maintenance job? No problem, here this is my place, I can arrange your post. After all, you belong in the garbage. Michael replied, "James, we came here to register in FA."

He turned to me, "what the hell? This person coaching the old college students to face my team and others? Hey loser, this is not any silly competition. This is FA and trust me, just as I hammered you in the last match of your career, you will never coach again." And he walked away and I called him and told, "remember the kick on your face? The scar is still on your face. At that time, there was something to stop me from finishing you. Trust me, this time, one dirty play and you will be finished by me." I just left infuriated from there and I only knew one thing, I am not going to lose this competition at any cost. So I decided to up the level for my players. In my mind I decided to change the training by introducing the development tiers at different levels to maintain the fitness level of the players who are not in the main squad. I called upon the players and told them, "for two weeks, you will undergo intense training with proper diet. You will not be taking food from the mess. You will get refund for two weeks' food bills which you already paid and I want you to reduce calorie rich food and strictly no alcohol or beverages. If I ever hear even a drop of alcohol being drank by anyone or unnecessary food practices, you will be on the bench and I will make sure you will not step up on the pitch. There will be training for around 6 hours a day with 1 hour team talk about tactics and gameplays. The practice starts from today. Start with twenty rounds of running, one hour gym physical exercise and practice sessions drills and physio exercises."

Everyone was surprised about the announcement and I was telling them that, "these are the rules for your life's best opportunity. Use them and you will be successful or you will be garbage. The best players from this tournament will be selected by various clubs across India and even the National team calls await you and for me you must win this because I believe that you have been coached by me and I know I am the best coach, so you never tell me about not getting the proper coaching."

Every player was amused and I shouted at them, "will you do or let me make you do it?" Karan whispered, "what happened bro?"

I replied, "it's James, Karan." He told me, "bro twenty rounds is so much. They will be tired." I stopped him and said, "Karan this is mine and their biggest match. Once I have bottled it during my career. I don't want them also to bottle it. I can't do it to them. They are all more talented than me. I have to make them strong. I know what James will come up with against me." Karan replied, "what will he come up against you with?" I replied, "Raghu, he is their main man. I have to win this so let them practice and do their job." I knew in my whole career I have never been so ruthless. I was obsessed during that time to make players sweat with blood and I have seen them tired, with difficulty in walking. In my mind, I was filled with pain for suffering my boys but I knew I had to do it. I just gave them intense pressure tactics many of them were having injury consequences but I didn't care about it. To my surprise everyone was working as a team as I could feel their intensity. I don't know maybe my attitude have been reflected upon them. But there was still something big to worry about, Krishna and John. I don't know whether they will put on their best performance individually but as matter of fact, in a match if both are marked, without their chemistry team will suffer. And without much concern, I was looking at the awareness concepts as I taught my players about various tactics by showing them the brilliant tactical masterminds of great managers like, Sir Alex, Pep Guardiola, Jose Mourinho, Carlo Ancelotti. As they have seen tiki taka, defensive and counter attacking football, I believe that they can reproduce it on the field.

And yes, the day of the big competition was going on and Michael came and told Karan to give all the coaching videos of mine as he wanted to show it to some officials and Karan gave some videos. Yes, the news was out that I was about to face James in my first practice match. My most feared nightmare was standing in front of me. As we were doing our team talk, I went to the dressing room and told them, "this is the biggest step to our career and you know James's team will be very much aggressive. You have to play passing football." I asked as every time to have a look at both of Krishna and John and asked Ravi to make a free flowing pass through midfield and told them to pass through wingers because their wing backs will be attacking aggressively and so they will have to follow a flexible 5-3-2 to 4-2-1-2 with John as false 9. And at last, I have to take the final decision regarding captaincy and I know in my mind I never had partiality and I want to give captaincy to both of them but for an aggressive match I knew only one candidate was suitable, that was Krishna and after I said this, I saw what was going through John's mind but I tried to ignore that. The team was lining up and James was standing up against me and he said, "welcome loser, ready to donate a mega victory to our team?" The match started and it was a smooth start but as expected, James's side started playing aggressive football. Players were pushed to the limits and the most worrying factor was that Raghu was their captain and again he know how we became exposed at the back and what points will a player be out of position and exactly it happened as in counter attacks by opposition team. They were caught out due to the lack of positioning by Krishna and John as they were dribbling every time higher up the pitch and their front 3 and midfielders were all over us and they didn't find much time to score the first goal and I knew this was going terribly wrong as I was shouting in the side-lines to get back and not move further to Krishna and John but they were playing reckless. Then came half time and I called upon Krishna and John and told them, "Krishna stay before the centre line, don't go forward and John what the hell were you thinking? Moving forward covering the area for the striker, this is a strong defensive side with muscular people. They will hunt you down. Look for spaces and create chances for strikers and don't bloody shoot from 40 yards or out. That is not your game that is Krishna's game and we can't do it against them. Now we are 1-0 down." And the biggest problem comes now, as usual Raghu was bullying Krishna and his shot temperedness strikes again and there was a red card for him and he was off. Our chance of counter attacking reduced again and our players were physically dominated by them and again they score 2-0 with our one man down. After Krishna's sent off, John made some good passes to get a consolation goal but it was too late. The final whistle blows and the score was 3-1. I was bloody furious and James confronted me with Raghu and told, "Loser, as usual another loss against me." Raghu was telling me, "good selection of captain. Such a bloody short tempered one and thanks to him for one goal and thank you for giving your captain to us and we hope John will be our player soon right, Raghu?" Krishna raged on to James and told him, "can you say that one more time on my face?" And finally, I slapped him for the first time and asked him to go back to his dressing room. He rushed to the dressing room and James waved at me, "goodbye loser. Tournaments are done for you. See you at stadium maintenance." I was bloody infuriated not only by his comments but also due to the performance and I went to the dressing room and I shouted, "what in the actual f****** hell were you thinking at that field? Defence were total out of shape and forwards was the only better thing I found in this game and yet they lost some chances and once again I want to see our star players. Where are they? Krishna and John? First of all Krishna, do you call your game football or boxing? What the hell were you thinking by tackling Raghu from his back?" He replied, "coach, he was pulling me." I told him, "oh because of that you can kick him? You idiot!" John shouted, "coach it was his fault that we lost our match." I told John, "oh I was coming to you. You are the bloody disgrace of today's game! What do you think, I am a fool? If you want to join Raghu, you can leave my team and join them, you bloody traitor. And because of both of you and your captain complexes, I am stripping of captaincy from you two. Ravi and Felix will be the captains. Suddenly John says to me, "at least I am better footballer than you. You just pushed your teammate and opposition player at the end of the game and cost us your game and we as a team failed." Karan went to John and told him, "I will kill you idiot." I told Karan stop and I started speaking, "yes he is right. Who am I to teach you? A failed player, a hated team player by the whole college but you don't understand, losing a match for your teammates betrayal, how will that feel? And because of that only I always wanted to train you to limits. Gave you chances to have good food, standard exercises, standard boots equipment and gave the best in every thing and you repay that by giving me this shit. You don't understand how you feel when you lose a final by one of your perfect decision for the moment but your teammate made you lose your whole career. This is my last match as the coach and I will be just a caretaker and Karan will be the main coach and I left." Karan was explosive and he told them, "you fools will never understand him. Every time he puts you to exercise, he never sleeps at that time. He always thinks of you getting a better future. He was devoted to this team and John, he was planning to give you an opportunity to visit Sunil Chetri, to make you learn some standard footballing advices and how many of you know he is paying from his own salary to pay for physio team. And Krishna, when he slapped you at there, I only saw tears in his eyes, he was holding it back. You morons never deserve him. You can do whatever you like. You are well capable footballers, right? Do what you like." He rages out and shut the room. The whole dressing room was silent after that. I was not able to sleep that night. I told Karan, "you know bro, I saw the fierce captain Roy Keane and Patrick Vieira in Krishna and a mixture of Zidane and Pirlo in John. I wish what could happen if they teamed up. They will tear up any defences and I am sure of that but it's sad that this will not happen." Karan told me that it was late and he was leaving and Arundathi was also along with me and she came to me and hugged me and told, "everything will be alright. This is your nurtured players. They will never give up on you. I took her back to her house and I went to the bed and at morning I was sleeping at my bed and suddenly, a knock on my door was heard. I went to the door and I saw Krishna and John together outside saying that they were sorry and they would work for the team at all cost. "Coach, without you we are nothing. We need you. We are stupid players and we don't know anything." They started crying and I went to them and said, "it's alright. You are students, you learn by making mistakes." I asked them about the rest of the players and they pushed me to change clothes and I saw one of my life's best scenes ever, my players were working tirelessly and they were showing no signs of tiredness and the only thing they want was more and more training and I rushed on to the field and shouted, "boys, let's do one more round", and they were working more aggressively than me and Karan was coming to the field and told, "what is happening here bro? I have never seen them play like this." I nodded and said, "now this is my team that is going to win this tournament."

XI
Team bonding and build up

My team was born and they were going from strength to strength each day. The next practice match they thrashed the opposition 5-0 and they had registered 15 shots on target and John and Krishna were both on the score sheet and both of them had scored an absolute banger from distance. Krishna had an outrageous 30 yard goal and John had a brilliant free kick. But I didn't trust the captaincy yet to be given to them and Ravi was the captain. The group stages were brilliantly amazing as the team bonding was magnificent. They have shown some brilliant stuffs around the team, defensive wise and some brilliant stats in the assist chart and scoring charts as both our boys were doing the business and I was happy. Michael was telling me that both Krishna and John were on the minds of the Indian team selectors and I was more than happy for them and Michael emphasised me that I was also leading the charts for the Indian Team manager. For me, it was a happy news but winning this tournament was my priority as I was more obliged to the players. We slowly knocked down our opponents, each one by one and we cleared the knockouts and we were the only the sports college team in the group. And we went into the quarter finals with an attack minded mind, 4-2-3-1 formation and we were facing a defensive 5-3-2 formation team and I was telling them that they will try to sit deep and play on the counter attack and I advised them to play through balls and made them aware to get maximum penalty and free kicks around the box. The game was running smoothly and well and we were having different chances but was not getting them. I know this was about to happen because without the coordination between John and Krishna we will not be able to have a break through and I was ready to substitute when the time was about to end and go to extra time but thank god, out of nowhere Krishna had a shot from outside box that went in and I was relieved and then suddenly one thing that caught my eye, Krishna was protecting John not getting tackled as he was always pushing the man who was marking John and the final whistle blew and we were through into semi finals and everyone around the team was happy and I saw a glimmer of hope to bring their chemistry back through one thing. Suddenly, John called me and told me something in my ears and I told him he must go and John left the ground to meet Raghu. When he reached Raghu, he welcomed John by saying, "my star boy, you know what I have done? You will be thrilled to see him", and John went into a room and saw James and he says, "John right? I have seen your game, you are a brilliant player. Next season you will play in my team with a high salary but you have to just do one thing. Do not play well and next season you will be in Indian team and you will be captain." John stood up and said, "with all due respect sir, I don't do contracts with traitors." Raghu raised his voice against John, "how dare you?."

John replied, "wait Raghu", and told James to take his phone and he attended the phone and it was me on the other side talking to him and I said, "it's a shame I guessed your move and told John to go there." James replied, "you don't know me." I replied, "I don't want to. I just want to tell you one thing, be prepared with a coffin because my boys will not thrash you but it will be a demolition."

Even though I told him in anger I knew in my inner mind there was a big issue between Krishna and John I have to fix and semi final is the perfect stage as we were not facing a strong team in semi's and even though they were error prone and stupid at aggressiveness, I decided to train them with aggressive attacking. Then it was a training off day and I saw Arundathi at outside ground and I asked her, "why are you here?" She replied, "you did not know?" I shook my head and she replied, "it's February fourteenth, Valentine's day you idiot." I told her, "no come on, Arundathi I have to plan some stuffs."

Karan interfered by saying, "what's your work? There is nothing to be done. Me and my boys will do the work. I think chief coach requires a day off, what do you think, boys?" Krishna told, "yes coach." I shouted at him, "go and train you idiot." I looked at her and told, "ok, I will come", and I went with her that evening. She told me, "after you become Indian team's coach, my dad is now impressed with your position and he is planning for our marriage." And yet again it was happiness all around me.

I told her, "I will win this for you, my players and for me." After my day off, the penultimate stage of the game came and I went to dressing room and told them regarding tactics and positioning and I ended up by saying, "you guys were playing brilliantly till now. I know you will win it comfortably but don't be overconfident. Play your game." Before entering the pitch I called John and told to attack aggressively. He replied, "that's Krishna's game, right?" I told him, "but today you have to play it."

Krishna came to me and I said, "do what you always do, protect John and score." Krishna looked surprised and laughed at me and said, "I will coach." After seeing the laughter, one side problems were over and now other side was yet to come and due to their poor defense, we took early lead and as expected, the time came and John fouled one of their players at a crucial area and due to the bad mentality of their team, everyone was having a go at John from the opposition team and Karan asked, "should we interfere?" I told him to observe the pitch carefully and the magical moment happened then and there. When Krishna saw John was pushed down he rushed to the opposition players and pushed them away and picked up John and said, "Come on, bro, stand up. They will do nothing."

Even though both my star players received yellow, I could see the surprise on John's face and he looked at me and I know what was the meaning of that look. He now knew why I selected Krishna as the captain of the team. We were leading 1-0 towards the end of the game and I saw Krishna shouting John's name and he just puts a brilliant lofted pass into the feet of John and only thing John had to do was to connect the ball with the feet and 2-0 to us and the whistle goes. We were into the final and everyone was happy around us, embracing each other and now I knew what to do for the finals and a way to develop chemistry between them.

XII
The Big Day

For the finals, the practice was going roughly and I knew I had only one issue to solve for the team and I had to do it after the training. I asked John and Krishna to stay back and I told them, "you know you are the most talented players, even more than me. You both understand the game very well and the call to Indian team is sure for you guys but John, did you ever know that he used to protect you from your marker and mask him from you and Krishna, I know you already know that but do you know John always looks at the left before passing, looking for you around the pitch. Both of you loved to play with each other but never admired each other, never complimented each other. You know Krishna, you have the talents of Vieira and Keane and John, you have the skills of Zidane and Pirlo. Imagine these players' skills being delivered to the pitch all along. You know I will be waiting to see that and for one thing, I have decided to make John as captain tomorrow. Rest is depended upon you."

It was the final day of the tournament and it was all down to this and I was ready for the pep talk. "I know we have already lost embarrassingly to this team but I know you all are brilliant footballers and trust me, you know much better than them and you are better players. Give your best because if you lose by giving your best, it's not a problem. Always try for a goal every minute. I just want to tell you one thing, I have already lost one final, don't lose it because it's not worth it. You are the best on the field, so be the best. Don't ever think about the size of them, it all depends on the mind power." Krishna was waiting outside and he asked, "will John be the captain of this game? If John becomes the captain, my whole work was wasted." James entered between and told, "of course he will be the captain because he is a person who wants to be the best. Your team player theory will not work there." Suddenly James's laughter face turned into a gloomy one as he saw John with the arm band and he removed it and he put the arm band around Krishna's arm. Increasing my happiness, for the first time, they did a high-five and I turned to James and asked, "did you bring a coffin? Because it's not going to be a murder, it's going to be a war on the field."

Even before entering the game I knew the result. As I said earlier, I saw the Keane, Vieira, Zidane, Pirlo combination on the field and trust me it was bloody beautiful. The ball was flying and James's team had not even scored a single shot on target and the passes completed between John and Krishna were the highest pass exchanges done by players in the whole tournament. And the goals were coming from strikers, John, Krishna and the last goal that sealed our victory was a brilliant free kick on the last minute which Krishna was taking. The free kick and a cheeky pass to John at the near post and I knew the only area John was stronger was near post shots. He blasted it into the net and yes, the whistle blew and at last, the victory was ours. I saw a infuriated James and I smiled at him and I don't know how this feeling was like, beating the best team in India by 4-0. As soon as I knew both Krishna and John were in Indian team, for the first time in my life, I received the trophy and that was a special feeling which no one could express. I couldn't move and didn't know what to do. I looked at the stance and saw Arundathi smiling at me. There was positivity all around .Then my ultimate wish was granted, I became the best manager of the tournament and every dream was coming true for me and it was all going to be a happy ending.

The players and everyone was celebrating and the day which I never will forget and for my ultimate wish was about to be fulfilled as we were waiting for the announcement of India's Manager for football team and failure never left me. The announcement came which showed James as India's Football manager and I was shocked. Michael was rushing into FA along with coach Roshan and they started enquiring and they told Michael that being blacklisted as a player was their problem and the clean record of James was more than enough for FA. But it was just their excuse and again failure has lashed upon me. James came to me and said, "hey loser, I told you. You can't win over me." Coach Roshan lashed upon him and told, "you always cheated and trust me, you will never be a successful coach." James replied, "poor old man! Ultimately you are the only factor that prevented him from success." Michael was rushing towards me and he handed over the phone to me and I was shocked to hear the news and I called Karan and told the information and I rushed to see Arundathi. I told her, "I am close to getting a big job give me three months that's all I'm asking."

"Arun no, you don't want to go we can sort out from here you should be here to talk to dad."

"Just hold this up to three months, trust me. This is something big. When I reach there, I will inform you." When I was leaving she said, "take care, I will be waiting for you." I replied, "I will come for you as soon as possible."

While leaving from India to Spain, I informed Karan to tell the news to Arundathi before one month but I don't know whether he told her this or not.

So, the foreigner asked me, "what was the news that you want to share?"

Suddenly, the airhostess came and told that we have to evacuate flight. "You should leave." The foreigner was like, "anyway, I think you only have three hours to marriage, you have to go." I looked at my watch. I was late and I only had a few hours before marriage and I was rushing after the check in and there I saw Karan and coach Roshan. I went to them and hugged them and I saw two of my former players, John and Krishna. They told me, "so happy to hear the news, coach." "Thank you, boys! I have seen you two players' performances, it's impressive." I suddenly said to Karan, "we have to go to Arundhati's house." Karan replied, "wait bro, we can go there after some time." I asked, "what bro We have to go fast. Take the vehicle." I realised that something was wrong with them and when I reached Arundhati's house, I went straight to her room and I was shocked to see her and James hugging each other. I called her and she replied, "Arun when did you come?"

"Why did you ask me to come to see you?", I asked. She replied, "when I thought so much about our relationship, you were not at all involved in me and you were never having any stability. So I couldn't wait another 10 years for you." I asked, "did Karan not tell you anything?" She replied, "yes, but a job in some place means what? How would I know if you will have a stable life? Anyway, I wanted to be more practical and someone's enquiring me, I have to go." James came to me and said, "sorry loser, bad timing." I couldn't speak a single word to him. I just came out of house, disgusted and betrayed. I asked

Karan, "why bro? Why didn't you tell her about my job?" Karan replied, "for what bro? After you left, she was no longer yours. Her mind was moving towards James only and when I went to tell her about your job, she was not interested in hearing it because she was more into him and not you. She is not your old Arundathi. She has changed bro and I don't want her to like someone who earns more money. She is not someone who likes your character. She now loves fame and money more than you." I replied to him, "its ok, bro. Anyway, I always felt that she was never destined to be mine and I am happy for her to choose a better life and I want you to give her this as a wedding gift." My phone was ringing and it was club official and I told them I am coming to them. I asked Karan to drop me at airport and I left to Delhi.

That evening, Karan gave her the gift and asked her to open and when she opened it, to her surprise, there was a new feed video tab which showed sporting Portugal and Karan asked one person to switch on the television and Arundathi was shocked to hear the news and it said, "Arun became the first Indian to manage the Portuguese club Sporting Portugal which is owned by the star player Cristiano Ronaldo and the private unveiling and press conference is going to be done by Portuguese star in Delhi." Karan told Arundathi, "I wanted to tell you that always but you were never listening and you were completely blinded by his money and fame and you suddenly lost belief about Arun's ability. And I never want Arun to have a girl who always wants money in her life. I want a person who loves him the most and now for sure he will get a lot better than you and trust me, you made this mistake. Arundhati's face was filled with bitterness and sadness. Then Coach Roshan turned to James and told him, "you can never stop him, boy.

He is far better than you. Please understand now that you cannot hold anyone's talent anytime." James was not moving or not speaking a word as he was terrified by this news and he couldn't contain the frustration he has in his mind. Before leaving Coach Roshan turned to Arundathi and said, "you will never understand him, never ever."

XIII
Epilogue - End of a great saga, time to begin a new one

There will always be something that changes you in your life. For me, it was everyone around me. Everyone around me helped me change to the level I am today. There was Michael, James, Coach, Karan and Arundathi. For me one phone call changed my life. Michael had already took my coaching videos and stuffs and was working with them and someday he had sent this to an International Agent who was Gregory Mendes, the agent of Ronaldo. He saw my videos and Ronaldo was looking for a fresh face as a manager and as sporting director. That day, it was Mendes who called me and said he was the agent of Ronaldo and he wanted me to be the manager and sporting director and he told me now Ronaldo will speak to you. Suddenly, my heart beat had stopped. The moment a diehard fan always wish for was going to become true. That day, I heard the voice from him. "Hola, my friend. I want you to join my club and we will have a contract discussion and players meeting in Spain. So, I want you to be here. Mendes will arrange everything. So, are you ok with that?" I was suddenly shocked and I was searching for a word, yes, as even three letters were difficult to find. Now I don't know destiny brought me here. I have lost everything in my life, the love of my life, my player career but for a person who wishes to be part of a game can never be turned down. He will always become the great. Now for me, there are my parents, my sister and Karan waiting for me at the unveiling ceremony and towards my left, I am standing with my idol Ronaldo.

Like the great quote "Talent is worthless unless you work hard". I don't know whether my life's destiny is over or will be there another saga to continue…. Let's all hope for the best!

…THE END…